Laptop Bug

and

Rip, Rip, Rip!

By Cath Jones

Illustrated by
Marcela Dugont

The Letter L

Trace the lower and upper case letter with a finger. Sound out the letter.

Down

Down, cross

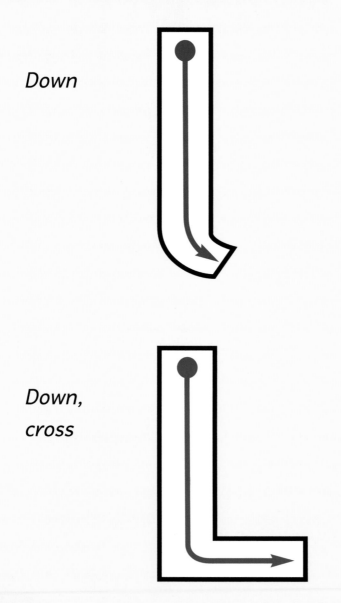

Some words to familiarise:

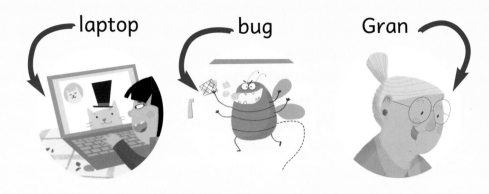

laptop   bug   Gran

High-frequency words:

to   go   the   no   is   a   in

Tips for Reading 'Laptop Bug'

- Practise the words listed above before reading the story.

- If the reader struggles with any of the other words, ask them to look for sounds they know in the word. Encourage them to sound out the words and help them read the words if necessary.

- After reading the story, ask the reader who got rid of the bug.

Fun Activity

Make your own bug out of pipe cleaners.

Laptop Bug

Can Kim get her laptop to go?

No!

Can Mum get the laptop to go?

Can Dad get the laptop to go?

There is a bug in the laptop.

Can Gran get the laptop to go?

Yes, Gran can!

The Letter R

Trace the lower and upper case letter with a finger. Sound out the letter.

*Down,
up,
around*

*Down,
up,
around,
down*

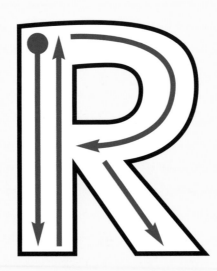

Some words to familiarise:

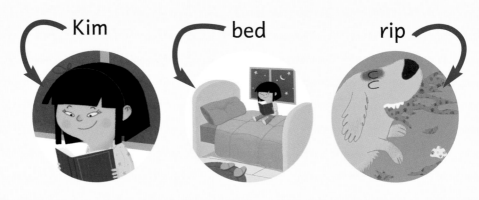

Kim

bed

rip

High-frequency words:

has a no is in

Tips for Reading 'Rip, Rip, Rip!'

- Practise the words listed above before reading the story.

- If the reader struggles with any of the other words, ask them to look for sounds they know in the word. Encourage them to sound out the words and help them read the words if necessary.

- After reading the story, ask the reader what happened to Dog's bed.

Fun Activity

Discuss other places Dog could sleep.

Rip, Rip, Rip!

Kim has a bed.

Dog has a bed.

Rip, rip, rip!

Has Dog got a bed?

No!

Kim is in bed.

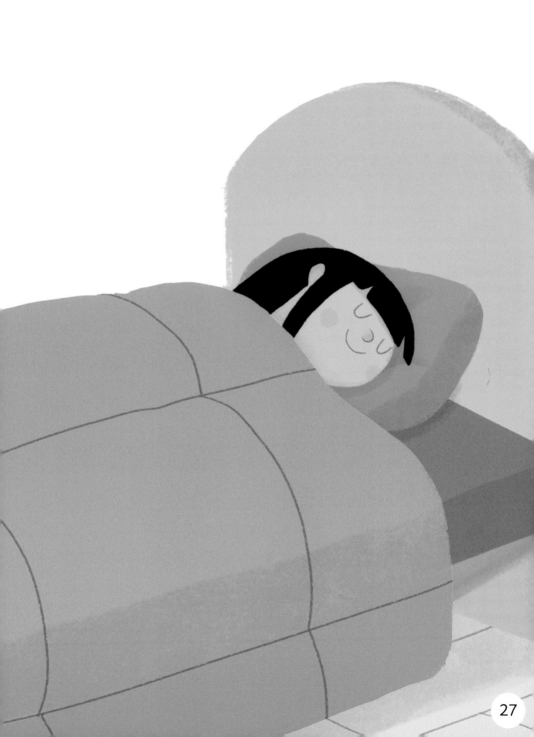

Dog is in bed!

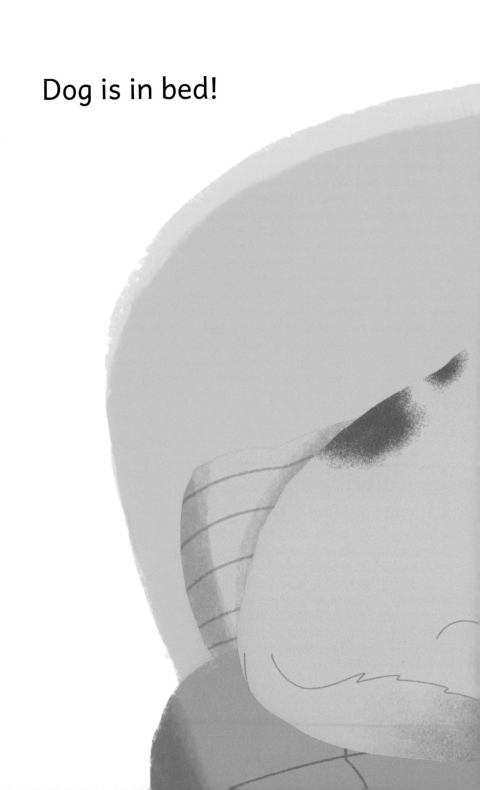

Dog is in Kim's bed.

Book Bands for Guided Reading

The Institute of Education book banding system is a scale of colours that reflects the various levels of reading difficulty. The bands are assigned by taking into account the content, the language style, the layout and phonics. Word, phrase and sentence level work is also taken into consideration.

Maverick Early Readers are a bright, attractive range of books covering the pink to white bands. All of these books have been book banded for guided reading to the industry standard and edited by a leading educational consultant.

Pink

Red

Yellow

Blue

Green

Orange

Turquoise

Purple

Gold

White

To view the whole Maverick Readers scheme, visit our website at www.maverickearlyreaders.com

Or scan the QR code above to view our scheme instantly!